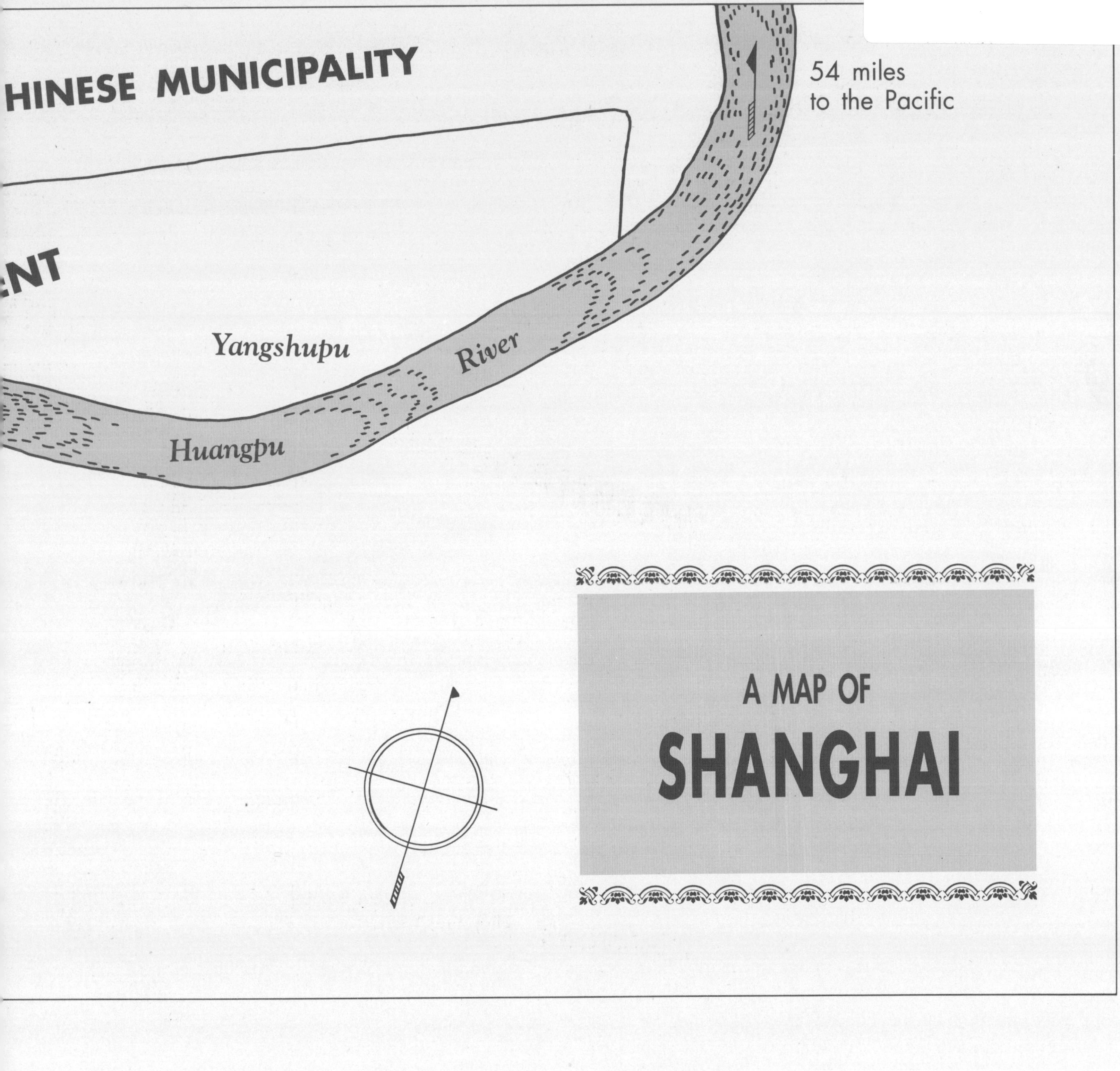
HINESE MUNICIPALITY
ENT
54 miles
to the Pacific
Yangshupu
River
Huangpu
A MAP OF
SHANGHAI

SHANGHAI
A Century of Change in Photographs
1843–1949

Lynn Pan
with Xue Liyong and Qian Zonghao

Hai Feng Publishing Co.

SHANGHAI
A Century of Change in Photographs 1843–1949

Editors: Lynn Pan
Xue Liyong and Qian Zonghao

Art Editor: Ki-Coo Seto

Published by: Hai Feng Publishing Co.
Rm. 1502, Wing On House, 71 Des Voeux Road, Central, Hong Kong

Colour separated by: Cheong Ming Production Company
Rm. 518, Block B, Metrople Building, 430 King's Road, Hong Kong

Printed by: Midas Printing Limited
5/F., Unitex Bldg., 100 Texaco Road, Tsuen Wan, Hong Kong

ISBN 962-238-171-5
HF-145-S

First edition 1993
Published & Printed in Hong Kong

SHANGHAI

A Century of Change in Photographs

1843–1949

Introduction

ONE HUNDRED and fifty years ago, in 1843, the great city of Shanghai was opened up as a treaty port. Indeed, for a hundred years, from 1843 to 1943, it was the supreme exemplar of that historical genre. Like Hong Kong, that other great port on the China coast, the Shanghai portrayed in these pages represented a foreign foothold won for Western merchants by the Nanking Treaty, the agreement which ended the first Opium War; it represented the first door opened into China by British mercantile interests and power.

A door is a meeting point, a place of encounter —in this case all kinds of encounter, between peoples and cultures, between stages of civilization, between ways of thought and ways of life. During the hundred-odd years spanned by the photographs in this book, Shanghai was an arena for encounters more varied and vivid than those experienced by any other city in the Far East.

Its very situation, on the banks of the Huangpu River, near the mouth of the Yangtze, was a meeting point between land and sea. Indeed, the very existence of Shanghai was bound up with water. The first denizens were fishermen and seafarers, and today's container ships are yesterday's seagoing junks and river barges. To this very day, the tang of a sailor's town hangs about some back alleys of Shanghai.

Shanghai began to live by its coastal and maritime commerce early in its history, and as far back as 1265, six centuries before it became a treaty port, a Superintendency of Foreign Trade was established there. It was from Liujiagang, a harbour to the north of Shanghai, that at least two of the spectacular fifteenth-century armadas of Admiral Zheng He began their expeditions to the coasts of Southeast Asia, India and Africa. And it was upon the trading junks of Shanghai and other southeastern Chinese ports that these *tours de force* of seamanship were founded, seamanship whose scale the world had never seen before.

To take to the sea is to look outwards, and if the mental horizons of the Shanghainese were wider than those of their landbound inland peers, this was partly because theirs was a port city, on the outer bounds of geography and experience. For such a city, openness to the outside world was all, and Shanghai's fortunes have indeed waxed and waned with the amount of overseas trade and travel countenanced by the ruling power in Peking. The old Chinese conflict, between ancient and modern, between extroversion and introversion, between nostalgia and progress, was one that shaped, and continues to shape, Shanghai's destiny. When, in 1533, the Ming court turned its back on the sea and prohibited overseas trade and shipping, Shanghai's merchants languished and the port with them. Though the ban did not end private seaborne trade entirely, this had to be conducted illegally, often in the form of piracy, which was usually but inaccurately attributed to the Japanese. In fact many of those named *wokou*, "Japanese pirates," in the Chinese records were Chinese crews and captains, goaded into buccaneering by the imperial ban on trading. These men might well have been traders had they not had to become pirates.

In the succeeding dynasty, the Manchu (or

Qing), the port of Shanghai was set back by the forced evacuations of the 1660s, when the court ordered the coastal population to be moved inland, behind a patrolled barrier, so as to deny mainland replenishments of food and manpower to the anti-Manchu resisters on Taiwan. Those were moribund days for Shanghai's seagoing traders, whose business all but withered; and it was not until the coasts were unsealed some two decades later, when Taiwan had been brought under full Chinese rule, that Shanghai's shipping could come back into its own. The port thrived, and even before the British flag was raised over it, Shanghai had become one of the world's greatest ports, with a forest of masts and a volume of shipping equal to or greater than London's. It is certainly not true what many foreigners have claimed, that the place was nothing but a sleepy village on a mudflat before they came; Hong Kong, that other prodigy on the China coast, may indeed have been conjured out of barren rock, but when the treaty powers turned Shanghai into a world-class city, they were building on far sturdier foundations.

So the treaty port was not founded *de novo*, but established on earlier maritime traditions. Yet Shanghai would not have been Shanghai without the treaty port experience. We shall never know if Shanghai's flowering could have somehow come from within, but still it is hard to imagine it fulfilling its destiny without the stimulus of Western enterprise and methods. If the sea offered a fructifying encounter of one kind, the coming of the foreigner offered another. To be a port was good for business, but to be a treaty port was better.

How Britain, France, America and Japan extracted rights and privileges so that foreign trade with China could prosper under foreign law, how they established foreign enclaves so that Shanghai became not just one city but three—the Chinese City, the International Settlement, and the French Concession, each with its own administrative, legal and police systems—are oft-told stories. For about a hundred years, Shanghai duplicated the styles and institutions of the colonial entrepôts of the British Empire in India and Southeast Asia, entrepôts such as Bombay and Singapore. By way of illustration, consider the use of words like "bund," "shroff," "chit" and "tiffin"—words of Anglo-Indian or Indian origin. Consider the Club, the gaol and courthouse, the racecourse, the amateur dramatic society, the turbanned Sikh policemen, the Freemasons, and those Parsee merchants who were always to be found in a British colony. It was by way of British India (and the cotton and opium trade) that Sephardic Jewish families like the Sassoons came to Shanghai.

There were Ashkenazi Jews as well, chiefly Russian émigrés arriving via Manchuria (China's northeastern provinces), their numbers cresting in the aftermath of the October Revolution of 1917 and the Japanese occupation of Manchuria in 1932. There were German, Austrian and Polish Jews, as many as 18,000 of them, refugees from Nazism finding an asylum in the International Settlement, the only landfall in the world to admit people without papers or a visa. Shanghai was nothing if not polyglot. Anyone who found himself in Dixwell Road, say, would hear more than a snatch of Japanese, the mother tongue of the city's single largest foreign community, whose size had grown to twice that of the British by 1920. It was thanks to the Japanese lead that so many cotton mills could be heard clack-clacking away in the city's industrial districts.

Of course the symbolism of the foreign presence goes beyond the city's cosmopolitan character, for behind these foreigners lay far grander themes. They congratulated themselves on being agents of progress, urging the Chinese to change their backward ways; "Be like us and you will succeed," they seemed to be saying, the prosperity of their banks and trading firms, the efficiency of their municipal services and the scientific superiority of their missionary teachers driving the point home. The achievement of material prosperity is never without its social and philosophical underpinnings, and the buildings of the Shanghai Municipal Council, the custom-house, the China United Assurance Society, the Hongkong and Shanghai Bank and the like were not just buildings but (to quote from Rhoads Murphey's book *The Outsiders*, 1977) emblems of "the Protestant ethic, the sanctity and freedom of private property, the virtues of individual enterprise, the power and self-satisfaction of private capital, and the battery of techniques which had burgeoned in the West to carry on the business of this new kind of world: stock companies, agency houses, trading firms, banking and insurance facilities, legal safeguards for the protection of enterprise and property, steam and steel, and the revolution in transport which underlay the new economic growth."

For a hundred years, the foreign enclaves offered themselves as models of modernity. A hundred years of such growth, such expansion of material, spiritual and intellectual capital! The vitality was in the new encounter—between indigenous and foreign, provincial and cosmopolitan. The foreign enclaves were by no means islands, separated from their Chinese surrounds by unbridgeable seas. There was public, commercial and social mingling, and out of that mingling came something we might call "treaty port Chinese," a creature whose detractors named "Yangjingbang," after the creek that formed the border between the International Settlement and the French Concession. Yangjingbang speech was pidgin, Yangjingbang ways were a hybrid of Chinese and foreign. The earliest generation of "treaty port Chinese" were the wealthy compradors of foreign firms like Butterfield and Swire and Jardine, Matheson and Company. These men made old-school Chinese hackles rise by their adoption of Western manners, yet as the first Chinese to straddle the cultural divide their importance can scarcely be denied. They were the archetypes of a brood of modern Chinese whose urbanity was unusual because it was Chinese as well as cosmopolitan, and whose present-day incarnations are to be found sometimes in Hong Kong.

Shanghai was where the modern world began, where the seeds of Chinese capitalism first came to flower. It was a foretaste of what other Asian cities would be like in the next generation. The city pulsed with physical and mental vigour. By the 1920s it had emerged from a provincial sort of urbanity into true cosmopolitanism. Chinese everywhere, at home and abroad, looked to it as Americans to New York. No city in the Orient, not Hong Kong, not Canton, not

Singapore, not Tokyo, presented so exuberant an image of urbanity. Its style and fashions were copied all over the greater Chinese world, and though its opening to the West lagged Singapore's, for example, by more than two decades, Chinese settlers in the latter city readily acknowledged Shanghai's lead in everything.

In another sense, too, Shanghai was a Chinese New York. It was a Promised Land to the refugees from war or want in the provinces, people pouring into town in their hopeful thousands, filling the place with ambitious strugglers fighting for space and opportunity. It was an ethnic mosaic where not only Chinese and foreigners lived side by side, but Cantonese and Ningbonese, Fujianese and Anhuinese. These juxtapositions were yet another kind of fruitful encounter, sparking competition and enriching Shanghai's diversity. Many of the newcomers trod the well-beaten immigrant path of rags to riches, but not a few were wealthy already, families of the older, cultured gentry of the provinces lured to the city by its shelter of law and order. The Taiping Rebellion, the Japanese invasion, the civil war—all these were occasions for massive inflows, swelling the population from about 500,000 in 1852 to more than five million by 1949, and fuelling the city with not only cheap immigrant labour but fleeing capital.

Of the countless Chinese Shanghai absorbed over the years, some of the most successful and entrepreneurial were returned émigrés, the so called *huaqiao*, or "overseas Chinese," who had settled for a time abroad and who would no doubt miss the modern conveniences and lifestyles which their expatriation had accustomed them to were they to return to live in any other Chinese city. One distinguished returnee was Dr Sun Yat-sen, in whose home on Rue Molière (Xiangshan Road today), now a museum, the visitor may find many a Western memento, some no doubt attributable to his wife, the second Soong sister Chingling, herself the daughter of a returned émigré and educated in America. And it was a pair of Cantonese brothers from Australia, Guo Le (James Gock Lock) and Guo Quan (Philip Gock Chin), who started the Wing On Company in Hong Kong and Shanghai with much of the investment originating in the diaspora.

It was an incomparable place, too, for literary and intellectual immigrants, who came here to live not only because of the evident advantages of being close to the newspapers and publishers who would purchase their words, but who needed the metropolitan tolerance of unconvention, the bohemian ambiance, and, perhaps even more importantly, the safety and freedom from Chinese government control safeguarded by the foreign authorities. The southward "brain drain" from Peking and other northern cities in the late 1920s turned Shanghai into the literary and intellectual capital of China. Novelists, poets, playwrights, artists, littérateurs, columnists and scholars abounded, some of them profoundly engagé, others merely concerned to pander to the huge public appetite for scandal and tales of exposure. By no means all the works produced were first-rate, but even the frankly popular (the love stories of the "Mandarin Ducks and Butterflies" school of writing, for instance) showed that mass appeal need not preclude skill and creativity.

The Shanghai equivalent of the artist's garret was the *tingzijian*, a small, badly lit room above the kitchen at the back of *shikumen* tenements, humdrum terraced dwellings rapidly thrown up to house the periodic streams of immigrants. The hard-up writer or artist ate his dinners in cheap Russian restaurants, where they didn't mind you stuffing yourself with bread and *borsch*. Life was by no means easy, but still it was like a dream of liberty, the closest thing perhaps to living in Greenwich Village or Bloomsbury.

The talent, creativity and political engagement concentrated in Shanghai expressed themselves in a plethora of newspapers and magazines, in the revivified theatre and in the nascent cinema. The new plays and stage performances, hybrid descendants of traditional Chinese opera and European drama, found enthusiastic audiences in the new class of petty urbanites. Many of the playwrights wrote film scripts as well; and in their hands, and the hands of a new generation of directors, Chinese cinema was carried to astonishing heights of virtuosity, earning for Shanghai the apt epithet of the "Haolaiwu [Hollywood] of the East."

The leftwing streak in many of the best movies could be traced to the communists, who were behind the main studios and who, too, found the tolerance of the foreign enclaves much to their liking. Indeed it was in a house in the French Concession, in 1921, that the Chinese Communist Party held its inaugural meeting. And besides, where would the worker's movement find a following if not among Shanghai's teeming proletariat of poor immigrants?

On the docks, in the factories, there were the usual activities of labour union and secret society, the two sometimes hard to tell apart. In the French Concession gangsters ran the police force *and* the underworld—just as the Irish once did in New York. All this is perhaps in the nature of an immigrant town, an explosively growing one at that. A greenhorn stuck to his own kind, and a tie of sentiment and need bound him to the secret society favoured by those from the same hometown or natal province—the Red Gang (Hong Bang) if he was from Hubei, say, and the Green Gang (Qing Bang) if he originated in Wuxi. Gangs ran fiefdoms all over the city, the perfect locale for opium and other mob businesses. Shanghai had certainly more than its fair share of those vice businesses that are part of a burgeoning city. That was the seamy side of urban life. Most of the immigrants were lonely single males for whom the height of happiness was going upstairs in Fuzhou Road with a singsong girl from Suzhou. Prostitutes overran Shanghai, which is again as you would expect.

It was a louche city. All life was there—big city life, encompassing both the best of men and the worst of men. As big city dwellers—city slickers, you might say—many Shanghainese no doubt congratulated themselves on having escaped the provincialism of their country cousins. Wherever they might have originated, whether Ningbo or Suzhou, they were proud to call the metropolis home. They might not have abandoned their original identity, might still clump together with fellow townsmen in "native-place associations," but when they found themselves in the company of outsiders they were only too pleased to declare themselves Shanghainese.

Shanghai was a true "melting pot," blending migrants from "the five lakes and the four seas," as the Chinese expression has it, into a single overarching ethnic identity. It is hard to say who the original Shanghainese were; almost from the start immigrant had outnumbered native—out of every hundred people in the 1880s, for instance, only fifteen were indigenous—so that the question "What defines a Shanghainese?" could only perhaps be answered, the matter of language apart, by reference to abstract qualities such as cosmopolitanism and urbanity. If Shanghainese appeared to early European arrivals in China to be less xenophobic than most Chinese (certainly less so than the Cantonese, who had made their anti-foreign feelings clear enough in the Sanyuanli encounter in 1841, in which one British soldier had been killed and fifteen others wounded), this was probably because a Shanghainese regional nationalist would be a contradiction in terms.

The Shanghainese was seldom on the defensive, seldom less than thoroughly comfortable in his own skin, persuaded as he was that his was the yardstick whose top everyone wanted to reach. To say, as many commentators did after 1949, that he was a lackey of Western imperialists is perhaps to recognize that he was a willing participant in the hybridization of Shanghai's habits and thinking. Radical commentators would have us believe that the treaty port Chinese was that familiar figure of subject nations, the collaborator who aped the manners of his alien master and despised his own. But actually that figure was rare in Shanghai, for the Shanghainese understood better than his detractors that being modern was not the same as deserting Chineseness for Westernness; it was not the same as cultural apostasy. Indeed he showed himself to be as patriotic as the next man at moments of nationalist high tide in China, his heartbeat quickening in the nationalist protests of 1919 (the May Fourth Movement) and 1925 (the May 30 Movement), and in the war of resistance against Japan.

The war years were not uniformly dark, but Japanese occupation tarnished the civic make-up and dimmed the dazzle of the city. What it also did was to put an end to a chapter of Shanghai history, the chapter that had begun with the arrival of imperial Britain in the Far East. Bringing into being a world in which power would everywhere pass away from those who had held it, the war swept away foreign rights and privileges and returned the foreign concessions to the Chinese. It was a conclusion, but it trailed a pendant: the final transfer of authority from the Kuomintang to the communists. The communist triumph in 1949 was what ended the treaty port world once and for all. (The only place on the China coast where that world would live on, albeit in a much diminished form, was Hong Kong.)

The years leading up to 1949 saw Shanghai's young pouring their hopes into radical and revolutionary ideologies, egged on by the underground Communist Party. After 1949 a new generation grew up excoriating the temptations of Western orientation and the treaty port century. The treaty port experience was negated, so that it began to seem in retrospect to have been a huge illusion. It came to be selectively remembered, and even more selectively portrayed by its new official spokemen. Good and bad had been allied in Shanghai in its noontime, but now the bad alone was remembered, and the glamour of it all cheapened as mere tawdry tinsel. It is only since the change in the political orthodoxy in the 1980s that the Shanghainese have been able to revisit and revise the legends of their city's history.

It has been said that the Western legacy is easily expunged and had no enduring effects, in a place of the mass, inertia and historical depth of China, but the inheritors of that legacy, good and bad, are in Hong Kong, Taiwan and America. The "opening" of a China reanimated by a new sympathy to capitalism in the 1980s has allowed two versions of Chinese to come together—the home nation and the émigré one—in joint endeavours of many kinds; and it may be left to those émigré children of the treaty port experience, together with the new urban generation at home, to sweep Shanghai on to its next incarnation, and even perhaps to the fulfilment of its destiny.

FINALLY, a word about the photographs anthologised in this book. They have been selected to reflect the three encounters, of land with sea, of Chinese with foreign, of immigrant with immigrant, that were the gifts of Shanghai's geography, history and demography. Those were fertile encounters, as we have said, spawning a familiarity with, and an openness to, the wider world, as well as a metropolitan identity bursting the narrow confines of provincial ethnicity. But because, by their very nature, photographic images directly reflect only surface events and phenomena, much of our story has had to be carried by captions. So that they may evoke the background and deeper significance of each image, the captions are fuller than is usual in books of this kind, but even so they give a far from complete picture: practical considerations rule out the inclusion of many photographs, but in confining ourselves to the 205 included here, we were also guided by our predilection for narrative and chronological treatment. We could have chosen the pictures by theme, grouping them under such rubrics as architecture, street life, personalities and so on, but we have not done this for the simple reason that what it meant to live in Shanghai in the hundred-odd years spanned by this book cannot be grasped without an impression, at times urgent, of time passing and life changing gear at fateful moments. A sensation of chapters opening and closing, so necessary to our idea of the treaty port experience, can only be conjured forth, we feel, by looking at the pictures in a temporal sequence.

Acknowledgments

Thanks to: the family of Hugh Collar for allowing us to reproduce the family photographs (pages 104 and 139); the Hong Kong Museum of History, Urban Council, for a print of the Bund (page 95); Sarah Tucker Wideman for the loan of her picture of the class of '40, Shanghai American School (page 136); the Hongkong Bank Group Archives for prints of the bank (pages 62 and 63), Daisy Kwok for a portrait of her family (page 81), Kang Zhengping (pages 138, 142 and 144) and above all Sam Tata, for the use of his magnificent photographs of the fall of Shanghai (pages 147, 148, 149 and 150).

Thanks also to: Tess Johnston, Heinke Sievers, Oscar Armstrong, Grace Lau, Margaret Lee and Ang Yee for help of one kind or another.

SHANGHAI

If there is one image to suggest Shanghai's *raison d'être,* that image is sail. Sited on the banks of the Huangpu River about 12 miles from its confluence with the great Yangtze, and handlily cut about with creeks and waterways, Shanghai was and is above all a gateway—in a sense *the* gateway to China. Seagoing junks (*shachuan*) were calling at its harbour at the rate of 400 a week a century before the first European traders arrived. From the first, the exchanges of commerce were Shanghai's avocation.

Shipping was the staple of Shanghai, a great emporium of inland, coastal and maritime traffic. The Merchant Shipping Assocaiation, built in 1715 at Majiachang outside the East Gate of the city walls, was Shanghai's earliest guild. Here religious spectacles were staged to mark the birthday of the sailor's patron deity Tianhou, or Queen of Heaven.

Inside (*top*) and outside (*right*) the City Wall, whose shape is still discernible in the ring road (Boulevard des deux Republiques, now Renmin and Zhonghua Road) around the Old Chinese City. Torn down in 1912, the wall was erected in 1554 to ward off marauding freebooters whose mecantile impulses were denied legitimate fulfilment by the emperor's ban on direct trade. Keeping out traders–turned–looters, the wall may be seen to symbolize the reining in of Shanghai's maritime expansion by the imperial closed–door policy.

Temple to the City God (Chenghuang Miao) and the Willow Pattern Teahouse (Huxinting Pavilion), approached by a zigzag bridge. Chinese merchants in cotton textiles, Shanghai's pre-eminent industry, put up the money for the teahouse, used largely for business powwows. The European posing in Chinese dress on the bridge suggests Shanghai's hybrid character.

The Shanghai *daotai* (circuit intendant) presides over a case (*top*). Gong Mujiu, the first *daotai* to have "barbarian affairs" added to his duties, was a co-drafter, with the first British Consul Captain George Balfour, of the 1845 Land Regulations providing for the setting apart of an area—the British Settlement—in which British traders might lease land in perpetuity from Chinese owners. Chinese-foreign collaboration was greatly furthered by the *daotai* Wu Jianzhang, said to be the archetype of the treaty-port merchant-mandarin. While enriching himself in office, Wu Jianzhang also advanced the interests of fellow-Cantonese immigrants, appointing them as clerks and runners, and as bodyguards (*right*), the "Cantonese braves" who became "Red Heads" (rebels) in the Small Swords Rebellion in 1853.

The first British Consulate, built in 1852 on land acquired by Balfour, was desroyed by fire in 1870 and a new building was raised two years later (*top*). Balfour was replaced by the more able Sir Rutherford Alcock. The French Consulate, which stood on Jinling Road East (*left*), was pulled down during World War II. In 1849 Louis de Montigny, the acting first Consul for France at Shanghai, founded the French Concession. The Chinese were to get on better with the French than with the British—only because, the latter were to claim, French authorities did not inquire too closely into Chinese revolutionary conspiracies and underworld activities.

The Bund, Shanghai's celebrated foreshore, at its junction with Peking Road, 1860s. To the left of the road is Jardine, Matheson and Company, the British trading firm founded on opium profits. The obelisk commemorates officers of the Ever Victorious Army killed fighting the Taiping rebels, the foreign names headed by that of General Frederick Townsend Ward, an American adventurer hired by the provincial governor Li Hongzhang (*see next page*) to raise a mercenary force.

Li Hongzhang (1823–1901), whose rise signalled new Chinese adaptations to the foreign presence (*left*). His obituary in the English-language paper the *North-China Herald* commended him as one who "had a working knowledge of the real relation between China and the outside world." Thanks to Li and viceroy Zeng Guofan, Shanghai became a laboratory of China's first forays into modernization, a series of "self-strengthening" reform measures in defence, industry and diplomacy partly inspired by Western example. The Kiangnan Arsenal (*top*), established in its outskirts, together with the Translators' and Interpreters' College (Tongwen Guan) attached to it, was part of an attempt to discover the practical secrets of Western power.

Rong Hong (*left*), better known as Yung Wing (1828–1912), was sent by Li Hongzhang to the United States to buy the machinery for the arsenal. A translator with the Shanghai customs service, Yung was educated in missionary schools in Macao and Hong Kong and was the first Chinese to graduate from an American university (Yale). Li Hongzhang backed his proposal for an educational mission to America and the first batch of thirty Chinese students (*right*) left Shanghai for Hartford, Massachusetts, in 1872. The youths learned to play baseball and Yung married one of the Hartford teachers, Mary Kellogg.

Well-heeled citizens, as essential to the make-up of Shanghai's citizenry as the destitute refugees driven by hunger and unrest to provide cheap labour for expanding industries. At the Taipings' approach, Chinese mandarins and merchants from the neighbouring provinces rushed into the foreign enclaves for safety, raising property prices from about £50 to £10,000.

Western businessmen dining with their Chinese compradors. As purchasing agents and the foreigners' native intermediaries, compradors were the bridge between Chinese merchant–guild commerce and Western free enterprise, and the first people to become modern entrepreneurs in China. They also set the trend towards the Europeanization of home decoration and living arrangements, being the first to acknowledge that some things Western, at least, were superior to things Chinese.

In response to the Western stimuli, Chinese commerce and banking began to spread their wings, shifting beyond the confines of the Old Chinese City to the northern side of the Suzhou Creek. Here, where nothing much had thrived before, the quickening of commerce called the Banking Guild (the building bearing a plaque) into being. Torn down in 1976, the guild house—its name prefixed by Beishi, "Northern Market," to distinguish it from its southern counterpart in the Chinese City—stood at the junction of Henan Road North and Tangku Road.

The Custom-house, 1857–1891 (*top*) and 1891–1925 (*right*), beflagged to mark the Empress Dowager Cixi's birthday on 17 November (she was 60 in 1894). The old Custom-house having been destroyed by the Small Swords rebels, and its services disrupted, the *daotai* Wu Jianzhang was persuaded to hand over the collection of customs duties to the consuls of Britain, America and France. Subsequently headquartered in Peking, the Imperial Maritime Customs had Sir Robert Hart, an Irishman who became the most powerful Westerner in China, as its inspector-general (*see page 138*).

Singers of the local *shenqu* opera (*top*). Of rural folk origin, sung in Shanghai dialect, the opera was initially known as "flower drum performance." Its lyrics were considered lewd, fit only for vulgar ears. Later it became more respectable, and enjoyed equal popularity with storytelling and stand-up comedies. The foreigners diverted themselves with drawing room comedies staged by the Amateur Dramatic Club, or ADC (*left*), formed in 1866 by foreign residents whose evening recreation had earlier been limited to wheelbarrow races up and down the Bund on summer evenings. Home to the ADC, the Lyceum Theatre was burnt down in 1871 and rebuilt in 1874.

With his taste also for outdoor recreation, the foreigner enjoyed himself with horseracing, paper hunts, shooting, excursions by houseboat to the country, cricket and rowing. For relaxation and company, he went to the Shanghai Club, 1861, rebuilt with Greek columns on the same opulent site on the Bund in 1910. Famous for the Long Bar, it pretended like comparable clubs throughout the British Empire to exclusivity.

The English penchant for gardens expressed itself in the Public Gardens, built on a reclaimed mudflat and landscaped by a Scots gardener brought out from Britain. Note the Chinese inside the gates (*top*). Until 1926 "natives" were not normally admitted, though no sign saying—in so many words—"Dogs and Chinese Not Allowed" ever existed. Chinese pose beside the Public Gardens' fountain (*left*), built to mark Queen Victoria's Jubilee in 1887. This and other parks were thrown open to the Chinese in 1926.

The Yangjingbang Creek, which divided the International Settlement from the French Concession. Because Chinese and Western merchants habitually talked business at a place near the creek, communicating in pidgin, "Yangjingbang" came to stand not only for pidgin English but, derogatorily, for any Chinese–Western amalgam.

Sampans on the Suzhou Creek, spanned here by the Henan Road Bridge. North of the creek was the American Settlement, which began life when the American Bishop William J. Boone, baulking at the high property prices in the British Settlement, established his Episcopal Church Mission in Hongkou. A haunt of sailors, gamblers and "the criminal class," it was amalgamated with the British Settlement in 1863 to form the international Settlement and a single government dominated by Britons, the Shanghai Municipal Council, was established for the two.

Pedestrian and vehicular traffic near a junction between the Old Chinese City and the French Concession. The rickshaw was first imported from Japan in 1874 by a Frenchman named Menard and was used in conjunction with carriages, broughams, sedan chairs, single-wheeled carts or wheelbarrows and bicycles. Electric tramways, with three classes of cars, appeared in 1908.

Every advance in technology imported into China had its first application in Shanghai. Where else in China would you find a telephone exchange? The Shanghai Mutual Telephone Co. started providing a phone service in 1900 and by about 1906 had a staff of 30 Europeans, men and women, including the supervisors pictured here (*top*), and 200 Chinese. Chinese and foreigners similarly worked alongside each other in the Chinese Imperial Post Office (*left*), established in 1896 to handle post bound for the treaty ports and initially supervised by the Maritime Customs. Six national post offices—British, French, German, Russian, Japanese and American—dealt with interantional mail.

The Shanghainese bought their vegetables from itinerant hawkers who travelled from street to street and door to door until a covered market was raised on Nanking Road in 1884. They bought their snacks—wonton (dumplings), fermented beancurd, eggs stewed in tea, mashed red bean purée and so on—from street vendors who attracted customers by their own special cry or ditty (*top*). Food abounded at the Sanjiaodi Market in Hongkou (*right*), which was to Shanghai what Covent Garden was to London.

It made sense for missionary teachers to concern themselves with girls, future mothers of the next generation of Chinese. Both the school for girls run by Chinese nuns at the Wangjiatang Virgin Mary Convent (*top*) and the Bridgman Memorial School for girls (set up at the West Gate by Dr Elijah C Bridgman, the Massachusetts Congregationalist who founded the periodical *Chinese Repository*) made it their business to impart the blessings of Christianity to Chinese girls. The first mission schools catered to Chinese orphans or children from poor homes, but later they became popular, indeed fashionable, amang well-to-do Chinese families.

Evangelizers and educators were not Shanghai's pre-eminent foreigners: businessmen were. At the top of the heap were the taipans, representing famous China coast trading firms like Jardine Matheson and Butterfield and Swire. They lived very grandly, and their style would soon be imitated by their Chinese compradors. Pictured here is the home (on Siccawei Road) of an English barrister, W V Drummond, born in London to the Reverend James Drummond of Highgate. Decorated by the Chinese emperor, he was chairman of large sugar and rubber companies in Perak, in the Malay peninsula, the capital for which was entirely raised in Shanghai.

The Bund and Nanking Road, 1893. To the left is the Central Hotel (southern annex of the Peace Hotel today), to the far right the Sassoon Company, built in 1928 by Ellice Victor Sassoon as the Sassoon House, part of which was the Cathay Hotel (the Peace Hotel of today). The names Sassoon, Hardoon and Kadoorie dominated the Sephardic Jewish community in Shanghai. The Sassoons, who originated in Baghdad and traded in Bombay before arriving in Shanghai, made their money in opium and property.

The Bund at Peking Road, 1893. "In What Region of the Earth is Not Shanghai Known," reads the banner raised to mark Shanghai's Jubilee (*top*), celebrated with a salute of 50 guns, illuminations and fireworks on 17 and 18 November, and processions by the Volunteer Fire Brigade and the Shanghai Volunteer Corps. The corps (*right*) was founded in 1853 with Captain Tronson of the Second Bengal Fusiliers in command to defend the foreign settlements against the Small Swords. It was drawn from many nationalities, including, after 1907, Chinese.

Shanghai celebrates its semi–centennial in front of the Holy Trinity Cathedral, 1893, the year the tower was added. The Gothic cathedral replaced the Holy Trinity Church, which began life in 1848 in a wooden building on land owned by Dent and Company. Sir Gilbert Scott's original design was toned down by a local architect named William Kidner to suit the more modest budget.

Hall & Holtz celebrates Queen Victoria's Diamond Jubilee, 1897. Bunting and illuminations apart, the day was marked in the Settlement by a service in the English Cathedral, a grand reception and a torchlight procession. The firm, started by Edward Hall and Andrew Holtz, began life as a bakery and grew into a sizeable retail business with its own taipan: Hall & Holtz Ltd., Provision Importers, Stationers, Wine Merchants, Furniture Manufacturers, Jewellers, Drapers, Tailors, Upholsterers, Furnishers, Bakers.

The German community welcomes Prince Heinrich of Prussia at the German Consulate, 1898. After inspection by the prince, the German Company of the Shanghai Volunteer Corps wore the letters "P.H. von P." on their shoulder straps. German interests were considerable and names like Siemssen and Carlowitz were well known in Shanghai.

The Manchu prince Zaifeng heads a mission to Germany to apologise for the death of the German minister Clemens von Ketteler, killed by rebels in the Boxer Uprising of 1900. Enroute in Shanghai in 1901, his entourage proceeds down Nanking Road, overlooked by the Town Hall (tallest building on right).

The International Settlement celebrates the coronation of King Edward VII, 1901. Though Shanghai was never a British colony, it often felt like one. A street, Avenue Edward VII, now Yanan Road East, was named for the English king. An American was later to say of the International Settlement that "It's about as international as the Tower of London or Westminster Abbey."

Thousands of Shanghainese were introduced to Western science and knowledge through missionary endeavours like the International Institute, founded in 1902 by Dr Gilbert Reid (standing at the back of the hall), who had arrived in China as a young missionary of 25 in 1883. Founded in Peking, the institute was forced to relocate in Shanghai in 1903 by the anti–foreign Boxer Uprising and was to wither away with Reid's death in 1927. The founder of the "Mission among the Higher Classes of China," Reid aimed his message at the educated elite.

Reid, seen here with other missionaries and the orphans they raised, had worked in Shandong, Confucius' province of birth, and was unusual in having a special regard for Confucian thinking. What would be better for the Chinese, he thought, than the Confucius–plus–Jesus way? The attempt to reconcile Christian and Confucian principles was reflected in the Chinese name of the institute: Shangxian Tang, "Esteem the Worthy [that is, Confucius] Hall." The name is remembered today in Shangxian Lane in Huaihai Road Central (formerly Avenue Joffre), where the institute once stood.

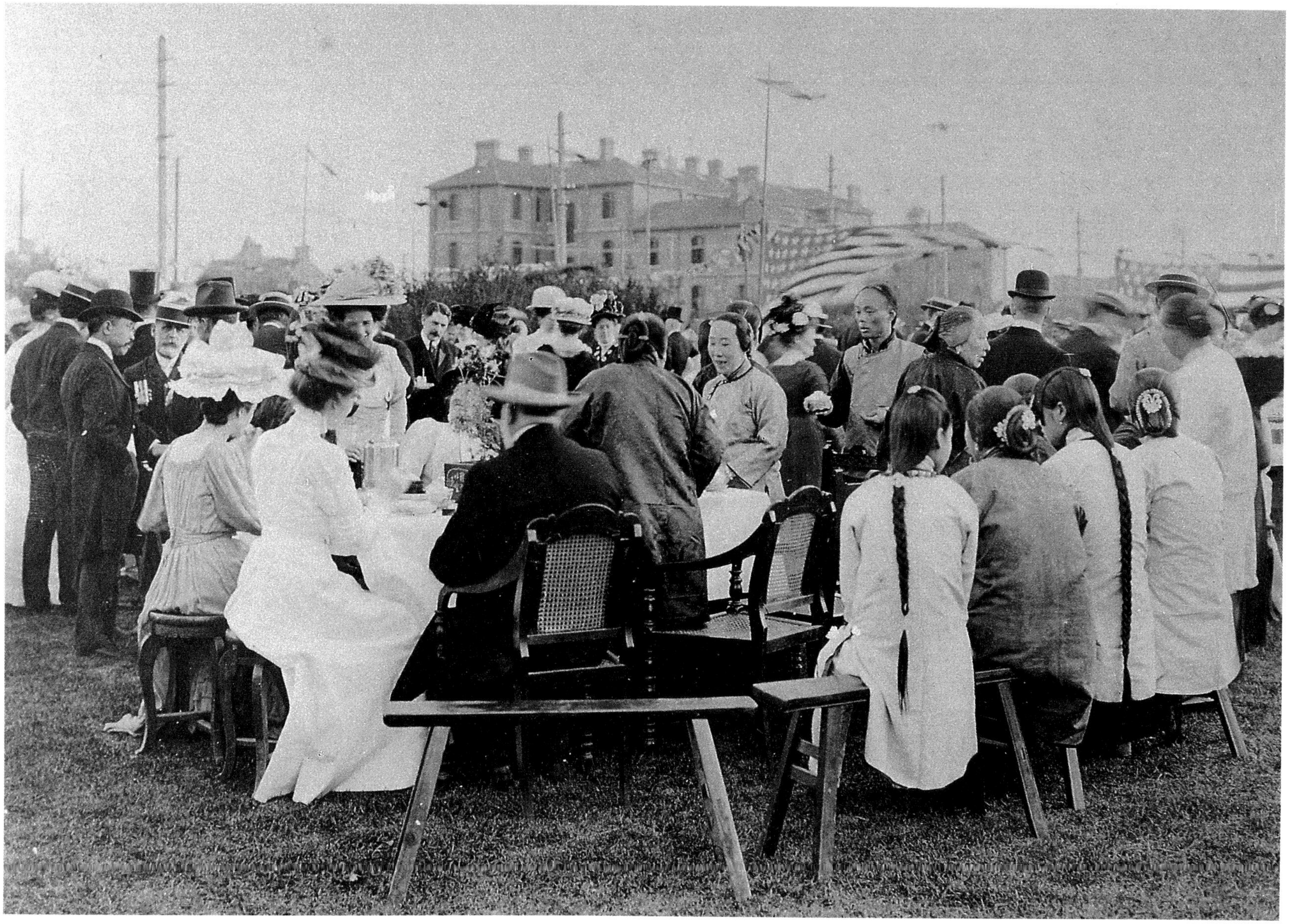

A reception held in the grounds of the Internatinal Institute, whose building was paid for by donations from China, America, England and other European countries, and had Chinese officials and gentry on its governing board. With Timothy Richard and Young J. Allen, well-known missionaries concerned to promote Western learning through translation and publishing, Reid became an enthusiastic propagandist for a reformed China and exerted some influence on leading Chinese reformers inside and outside official circles.

First Communion boys (*top*) at the St. Francis Xavier College for Boys, 1905. In missionary work American Protestants were supreme, but Catholic Shanghai was a French Jesuit preserve. The college was one of several educational establishments—another was the Aurora University—founded by French Catholics to advance their mission. it took in both foreign and Chinese students, and classes for the latter were taught in English. Many pupils stayed on to become teachers (*bottom*) upon graduation.

At the Jesuit settlement at Siccawei, Chinese children were given vocational training and taught crafts such as carpentry, carving, painting and embroidery. Pictured here is a convent class in spinning and weaving, an obvious choice of vocation in a city deriving much of its wealth from cotton mills and silk filatures. Of the latter's product, a 1900s commentator wrote: "No silk in the world can equal it in quality, brilliancy, and that subtle attribute, known to the trade as 'nerve,' responsible for the rustle so sweet to the feminine ear."

In 1889 a home for destitute children run by two women brought out from England was given money and land by Mr (later Sir) Thomas Hanbury, and amalgamated with a school for half-caste boys and girls to form the Thomas Hanbury School for Eurasians and Children's Home. Hanbury, an English businessman, had made his fortune chiefly from property. Opening on Boone Road in 1891, the school presently took in poor children of many nationalities.

Education was by no means a Western preserve. Nanyang College, Jiaotong University's predecessor, was given life chiefly by a powerful figure in Li Hongzhang's administration (*left*), Sheng Xuanhuai (1844–1916). In today's vocabulary Sheng would probably be called a "national capitalist." He presided over the most important of the *guandu shangban* (merchant–undertaking–under–official–supervision) enterprises, the China Merchants' Steam Navigation Company, founded in 1872 to challenge Western shipping in China. Another remarkable capitalist was Yu Qiaqing (1867-1945), a comprador (to the Netherlands Bank and the Russo-Chinese Bank) turned merchant shipping entrepreneur (*right*).

The main police station on Fuzhou Road. The Settlement was initially policed by consular constables and Chinese watchmen, but later it maintained a police force staffed by Westerners, Chinese and Sikhs from the Punjab (whose red turbans earned them the Shanghainese nickname Hongtou Asan, "Red-headed So-and-So.") The British Empire made Sikhs familiar in Shanghai and Hong Kong, where they are still to be seen outside jewellery shops and swanky hotels.

Women prisoners wearing the cangue, 1907 (*top*). Chinese administration of justice gave way increasingly to British and French in foreign Shanghai. From 1864 legal cases were tried before the "Mixed Court," an odd institution presided over by a Chinese magistrate and a foreign consular assessor (*right*). The court was resented by the Chinese as yet another extension of Western powers and jurisdiction, all the more so for the foreigners' enjoyment of "extraterritoriality," the right to remain subject only to the laws of one's own country rather than to those of China.

A singsong girl. Some were sold to Shanghai's countless brothels by kidnappers, others by impoverished parents from the country, particularly Suzhou. Singsong girls were inseparable from Shanghai's reputation as China's Sodom. "Flowers," as they were called, could be looked up in a guide or directory, or in books celebrating and ranking the 100 most famous. One guide divided Shanghai's "flowery kingdom" into *yaoer* (courtesans), Cantonese prostitutes, Japanese geishas and boy actors (who often doubled as male prostitutes).

Shanghai had a staggeringly lively sexual market, as befits a thriving sailor's port and immigrant boomtown. Chroniclers of the bordello culture celebrated famous Shanghai courtesans (*top*) in poems and illustrated limited editions, and periodically drew up "honours' list" of the best. Like clubs in the West, bordellos were places of male relaxation where opium might be smoked, a banquet might be held, and a game of mahjong played (*right*).

Huang Jinrong (1868–1953), or Pockmarked Huang (*top*), was chief of Chinese detectives in the French Concession's Garde Municipale and simultaneously a leader of the underworld Green Gang (Qing Bang) with interests in opium smuggling, gambling casinos, prostitution, bathhouses and protection rackets. Du Yuesheng (1888–1951), the godfather of Shanghai (*left*), epitomised better than anyone the peculiarly Shanghai mixture of fabulous opportunity, shady speculation, polictical skulduggery and pleasure in swank.

Broadway (Daming Road East today), to the north of the Suzhou Creek in Hongkou, an area which began flying the Stars and Stripes in 1854, some fifty years before this picture was taken. Broadway was an important thoroughfare by Hongkou standards, but not many residents from south of the creek would give it a second look. It formed the hub of what was to become known as Little Tokyo, the Japanese quarter. Their right to set up factories secured by the treaty which concluded the 1895 Sino–Japanese War, an increasing number of Japanese came to live in Shanghai.

A motorcar arouses curiosity in the Old Chinese City. The automobile arrived in 1902 in the form of two Oldsmobiles imported by a Hungarian named Leinz. Twenty-five years on, Shanghai would have some 8,800 motor vehicles, accounting for no less than half of China's total.

The coronation of King George V in June 1911 was an exhibition of British economic and political pre-eminence in foreign Shanghai (*top*). Another symbol of British power is the Jardine Matheson building at 27 The Bund, shown here with a crowd gathered in front of it to enjoy an evening's theatrical entertainment (*right*). The fortunes of this "princely hong," called Ewo in Chinese, were founded on opium. Headquartered in Hong Kong, Ewo became the greatest trading firm in China, with interests in shipping, insurance and cotton milling.

Mass at the Church of St. Ignatius, Siccawei (Xujiahui), *the* Catholic mission base in east China. Saving souls was Siccawei's most obvious business, but the Jesuit Fathers combined ecclesiastical work with running a meteorological observatory, an orphanage, a library, a printing press and schools where young Chinese minds were bent to the study of French and Latin. Nor was the dissemination of knowledge one-way; China was unfolded to Europeans through the scholarly monographs the Jesuits wrote under the series title *Variétes Sinologiques*.

A busy thoroughfare. The men's queue—the long pigtail of hair braided from behind the shaved forehead—was forced on the Chinese by their Manchu rulers, whose tribal hairstyle it was. Cutting off this symbol of humiliation became a gesture of Chinese patriotism. Beneath the placid surface of things, patriotic revolutionists were at work: risings were being plotted by the Kuomintang's precursor, the Chinese Revolutionary Alliance which Sun Yat-sen had founded in Japan, and by the radical student supporters of the Restoration Society.

The overthrow of the Qing began with an uprising in Wuhan on October 10, 1911. That was the trigger: city after city rose against the Manchus after that, Shanghai included. There, the Kiangnan Arsenal was attacked by the revolutionary forces with the help of merchant militia. "Shanghai went over to the Revolution without any fighting on November 4th," wrote an American observer. "The outward evidence was the appearance of white flags on all houses and shops, especially on Nanking Road."

Dr Sun Yat-sen (*second left*), his second in command Huang Xing (*seated to Sun's left*) and other comrades in arms in Shanghai (where Sun later made his home) after the 1911 revolution. Shanghai's money was essential to both the provisional government Sun formed and the political party (the Kuomintang) he headed. Sun was to marry a girl from a Shanghai family, Soong Chingling, the sister of Soong Meiling and Soong Ailing, his secretary.

Sun Yat-sen at a party given in his honour by the Sephardi Jewish millionaire Silas Aaron Hardoon (*seated right*), April 6, 1912 (*top*). The three women are (*left to right*) Sun's daughters Sun Yan, Sun Wan and his secretary Soong Ailing. Hardoon (*left*) and his Chinese (some say Eurasian) wife Luo Jialing liked to hobnob with Chinese dignitaries. He might have put up the money for the Beth Aharon synagogue, but he was hardly a pillar of religious society, and if any Jewish Shanghailander went native, he did.

In front of Arcadia Hall (Ankai Di, "the Mansion of Quiet Joy") in the famous Zhang Gardens, where you could stroll, sip tea, dance, eat, watch performances or drop in on an exhibition. You could even, if you were of a patriotic and idealistic temperament, plot the overthrow of the Manchus in the years leading to the revolution. Here Dr Gilbert Reid (*see page 32*) is pictured with the bearded Joseph Ma Xiangbo. Brought up Catholic, Ma was the founder of both French Jesuit Aurora University and the secular Fudan Unviersity.

The 1911 revolution had brought not regeneration but disorder. Profounder change was needed—the search for what that might be ushered in an intellectual and patriotic upheaval broadly termed the May Fourth Movement, a milestone of which was the events of May 4, 1919, when students met in Peking's Tiananmen Square to protest the loss of Chinese rights to Japan at the Versailles Conference. In Shanghai impassioned speeches were made by merchants and students at mass meetings, their anger expressed in strikes, agitation, the closing of schools and the boycott of Japanese goods. All these marked a new stage in Chinese consciousness.

Looking south from Sichuan Road, with Whiteway, Laidlaw & Co to the left, Weeks & Co to the right, and Hall & Holtz to the far left, 1915. A great commercial emporium, Shanghai was now a shopper's paradise. The place was enjoying boom times, seizing the exceptional opportunity for economic expansion offered by the First World War; taking full advantage of the decline of European imports and competition and the growth in world demand for raw materials, Shanghai's budding capitalists came into their own, ushering their city into its golden age.

The Wing On (*left*) and Sincere (*right*) department stores, which opened on Nanking Road in 1919, symbolized the emergence of a new generation of Chinese entrepreneurs, a new-style bourgeoisie which vigorously challenged the foreign domination of modern business. First set up in Hong Kong by Cantonese families who had made their fortunes overseas, these stores were part of an efflorescence of Chinese enterprise in the interwar period.

The Cantonese émigrés concentrated entrepreneurially as retailers, the Ningbonese as bankers, and those from Anhui province as pawnbrokers. Known by the character *dang*, painted in black on the white front wall, the typical pawnshop was located at a street corner and had two exits, so that if you bumped into an acquaintance there, you could always say that you had only walked through the shop to cut out the detour around the thronged corner. Though decidedly second-string to banks, as a moneylending institution pawnshops did their bit in keeping goods and money on the move.

Dock workers buy boiled drinking water, early 1920s. Boiled or hot water sellers were familiars of the city's petty trade. Their shops were called *laohu zao*, tiger kitchens, because their stoves burned so much firewood that it was as if one were feeding a tiger. They usually sold tea as well, and, come summer, would offer basins and water for a wash. Their charges were very low, their customers being poor migrant labourers with barely a roof over their heads.

"Wang Zanchun, Dentist," early 1920s, awaiting patronage at his stand, rigged up, as was usual, in the street. Such stands habitually displayed sets of teeth in a glass case and rows of decayed teeth successfully extracted from customers. To attract customers, some sounded a gong. Because the stands came shaded with awning, roadside dentists were known to locals as "Big Umbrellas."

Bibs, hats and belts for sale at a street stall, late 1920s. Shanghai sold everything, from French perfumes to herbal pear syrup candy, and catered to every income bracket. Because so much selling was done in the open, the streets buzzed with activity. Pavements were thick with itinerant cobblers. *fengqiong po* ("seamstresses for the poor"), pedlars of food, purveyors of junk, jugglers, portable lending libraries. One got things done quickly and cheaply because there was hardly a service trade that could not be found just round the corner.

A Cantonese teahouse in Hongkou. In a typical teahouse storytellers and balladeers entertained patrons, singsong girls solicited trade disguised as sweetmeat and watermelon seed sellers, "estate agents" (nicknamed "white ants") brokered deals between landlords and tenants, police detectives tapped gossip, and merchants and suppliers talked business.

Shanghai had two kinds of money, either the silver dollar, commonly called "Mex," or the tael, used for large transactions like land purchases. It had two kinds of bank, the modern sort familiar from London or New York, and the old-style *qianzhuang* or "native bank" dating back to the late eighteenth century (*top*). Shanghai was China's financial capital, and its citizens were canny manipulators of big money. The Shanghai Stock Exchange (*left*) began life in 1903, but the Shanghainese had been dealing in shares since 1882, when they set up the Pingzhun Securities Company. Spectacular booms and busts were an inextricable part of Shanghai's business life.

Much made the guests gasp on the gala opening day of the new Hongkong and Shanghai Bank building on the Bund on June 23, 1923: the eight columns of Sienna marble supporting the dome of Venetian mosaic, the 300-foot long marble counter in the central banking hall, the sheer magnificence of it all. It was an outward sign of an inner purpose, a visible totem of the whole ideology of capitalism. For seekers of profit, Shanghai combined the allures of a currency speculator's dream and a commercial and industrial powerhouse. The architect was Tug Wilson of Palmer & Turner; the brief, "Spare no expense but dominate the Bund."

Other banks were simply branch offices or agencies of British Empire houses, but the Hongkong and Shanghai Bank was a China coast institution. Established in Shanghai in 1865, one year after its opening in Hong Kong, it was to grow spectacularly and to wield enormous influence. Business with Chinese clients went through the bank's comprador, who would personally guarantee a loan (or, in the parlance of the day, "shroff the thing up").

Near the Sanjiaodi Market in Hongkou (*top*) and in many other parts of Shanghai, what gave pattern to Chinese housing was the lane system: most Chinese lived in narrow lanes or alleys, *longtang*, that led off at right angles from the long main street. In the old days entrances to lanes (*right*) were closed by gates. The lanes bore names with characters like *an*, "peace," *shou*, "longevity" and *de*, "virtue."

Closed to motor traffic, floored in cement, lanes were lined with *shikumen*, Shanghai's answer to "two up, two down." *Shikumen* were identical terraced brick tenement homes quickly and cheaply thrown up to house the city's growing population of poor immigrants. A typical *shikumen* house had a small open courtyard shut in by a cement wall reaching to the second storey, six rooms (three up and three down), a staircase at the back and, next to it, a low kitchen with a small room called *tingzijian* above it. Rooms were let and sublet, and a stock character in Shanghai lore was the rapacious Second Landlord.

Posing a sharp contrast to the hugger–mugger *shikumen* tenements were the grand villas of the rich. Set in spacious grounds on Avenue Joffre (1517 Huaihai Road Central today), Sheng Xuanhuai's (*page 38*) opulent home (today occupied by the Japanese Consulate) was infused with the style of gentlemen's residences in Europe. Just the bathroom would tell you that this was a place built for magnificent living.

The Shanghai War Memorial, unveiled on February 16, 1924 and representing the Angel of Victory, stood at the entrance to Avenue Edward VII and bore the inscription *"Ad mortuorum gloriam."* Because China had entered the war on the side of the Allies, all German and Austrian residents in Shanghai had to register in the Town Hall and to relinquish their rights of extraterritoriality. Foreign Shanghai had celebrated the Armistice by holding thanksgiving services in all the churches.

Refugees from the interior, probably from neighbouring Zhejiang. Shanghai was at the receiving end of large waves of migration from the neighbouring provinces of Jiangsu, Zhejiang and Anhui. War and natural disasters—floods in 1911, 1921 and 1931, for instance—impelled the influx, but so did opportunity and metropolitan allure. Immigration gave to the fabric of Shanghai its patchwork quality, its division by dialect and place of origin into ethnic solidarities—Cantonese with Cantonese, Ningbonese with Ningbonese, and so on.

Refugee migrant labour found ready if ruthless takers in Shanghai's burgeoning factories, its cotton spinning mills and silk filatures. There children little more than six years old were put on 12-hour shifts. Much of the work in the filatures was done by women and young girls, who were paid a quarter less than men for doing the same work (in 1929 half of Shanghai's industrial workers were female). Half of Shanghai's wealth stemmed from textiles factories, which employed more than half the labour force.

The 1910s were uniquely and incandescently a decade of capitalist flowering in China. With European energies absorbed by World War I, Chinese entrepreneurs expanded like fury into import–substitution manufacturing, helped by the decline of foreign competition, the increased world demand for raw materials and foodstuffs, and the raising of the value of the Chinese tael by higher world market prices for silver. First among the modern Chinese industries to expand was cotton, and Chinese fabrics and yarns became markedly more plentiful at home and abroad.

A working class family in Yangshupu (*top*), an area abutting the riverfront to the east and extending from Broadway along Yangshupu Road to the Settlement boundary. Home to mills, factories, engineering works, wharves, warehouses and worker's housing (*left*), Yangshupu was Shanghai's chief industrial section and the soil which grew its proletariat (30,000 of whom were textiles workers).

Coolies crossing a bridge, a generic Shanghai image (*top*). In 1920, a quarter of Shanghai's population, or 500,000 people, were working class. Among these poorly housed people (*right*), the Chinese Communist Party, established in 1921 in the French Concession, found an eager following. Their increasing activism expressed itself in strikes organized by communist cadres like the future statesman Zhou Enlai.

Anti-imperialist agitprop commemorating the May 30th (1925) Incident. Such rallies were organized by both the Nationalists and communists. The incident signalled the communists' success and a growing anti-imperialist mood, and marked the beginning of the end of Western power in China. The death of a Chinese factory hand in a Japanese-owned mill sparked demonstrations in which students were arrested. At an order by a British police officer, demonstrators were shot outside the Laozha Police Station. The Chinese downed tools in a general strike and the Municipal Council declared a state of emergency.

Billboards advertising American film and cigarettes. The cigarettes market was an arena of foreign–Chinese business rivalry. BAT (British American Tobacco Company) was supreme, until challenged by the post–World War I crop of indigenous Chinese tobacco companies—these rose from three in 1914 to 100 in 1929. The biggest of these was the Nanyang Brothers Tobacco Company; founded by the overseas Chinese Jian brothers in Hong Kong, it transferred its head office to Shanghai in 1919. The thrusting sales and advertising techniques it used to break into the market showed how modern and advanced it was.

Catholic efforts to minister to the poor ranged beyond the limits of the city. Catholics had converted more Chinese than had Protestants, but neither did well as soul savers; both did better as educators and social workers. Thanks to the May Fourth Movement, there was now a new resistance to them: an anti-Christian and anti-imperialist mood among the intelligentsia, who saw religion as yet another instrument of cultural imperialism and as a drag on China's modernization

The mounted American unit of the Shanghai Volunteer Corps rides down Nanking Road. The corps was mobilized as Chinese voices were raised against the foreigner, shouting slogans like "Cancel unequal treaties!" and "Restore all foreign settlements to China!" Strong resentment against foreign privilege needed only to be channelled into a revolutionary tide of anti-imperialism. This was whipped up by a triangle of Nationalists (Kuomintang), communists and Soviet advisers.

In early 1927 the Kuomintang armies of the Northern Expedition, a great nationalist movement led by Chiang Kaishek, were sweeping up from the south to seize Shanghai from the local warlords. They were awaited by 22,000 foreign troops and police, and 42 foreign warships at anchor. Suddenly the city was full of soldiers—Indian, British, American, French and Annamite. Ground for Chiang's capture of Shanghai was meanwhile being prepared by his allies in the united front, the city's communist trade unions.

Unease swept through the foreign enclaves: "The Reds are coming." In the event the struggle for the control of Shanghai did not pit Chinese against Westerners but Chinese against Chinese. In a betrayal of the highest order, Chiang moved against his allies in the united front and crushed the worker's movement in a bloody purge on 12 April. To the coup's success, the money of Shanghai's businessmen, the brawn of its underworld and the connivance of its foreign authorities all contributed.

Garden Bridge with the Astor Hotel (the oldest hostelry in Shanghai) and the Soviet Consulate, 1930. In the White Terror which followed Chiang's coup, the triangle of Nationalists, communists and Soviet advisers broke apart and the consulate was closed and did not reopen until 1933.

After the April massacre in Shanghai, Chiang (*top left, in uniform*) proceeded to make himself supreme. One important connection he forged was with the Soong family, contracting a bigamous marriage to Soong Meiling (*right*), the younger sister of Sun Yat-sen's widow, Soong Chingling. The wedding was celebrated in the four-leaf-clover-shaped ballroom of the Majestic Hotel, where a Russian orchestra played Mendelssohn and an American tenor sang "Oh Promise Me." He then brought in his brother-in-law T.V. Soong (*top, right*) to run the Kuomintang's finances.

Millions were squeezed out of Shanghai's moneyed class to pay for Chiang's military campaigns. Many kinds of entrepreneur made up that class. Immigrants from around Ningbo dominated the banking sector, but retailing was a Cantonese forte. Exemplars of the latter were the Cantonese brothers Guo Le, Guo Quan and Guo Biao (pictured here with his family in front of his home), founders of the Wing On Department Store. One-time émigrés in Australia, the Guos were profitably plugged into the overseas Chinese network.

The Bund, 1929. The city's "pride and glory," it stood as a statement of solidity and security—security in the sense of protection against violence and disorder (by the treaty powers' gunboats on the Huangpu River) on the one hand, and safeguards for personal rights, including rights of property, on the other. Few Westerners could have seen it as a precarious perch from which they would be swept away one day.

Race meets occupied prominent places on the sporting and social calendar of Shanghai. They were organized by the Shanghai Race Club, the major meets of which were held at its course on Nanking Road in May and November; and also by the International Recreation Club in Jiangwan and the Chinese Jockey Club beyond Hongkou Park. The horses were "China ponies" imported from Mongolia, though it was whispered that the occasional Arab was insinuated into the race.

Shanghai pedestrians on Nanking Road. Women wear the cheongsam, evolved from the straight, loose and ankle–length gown of earlier Manchu women. The end of the 1920s saw changes in style under the influence of Western costumes—the length shortened and the fit tightened. Men adopted the Western suit, which coexisted with the long gown. To have a Western suit made, it was best to go to a tailor from the Ningbo area, emigrants from which, particularly the town of Fenghua, dominated the profession.

Shanghai led the Chinese world in fashion. Models, pictured here being photographed (*top*), coveted the covers of a growing crop of illustrated magazines, themselves a modern phenomenon inseparable from Shanghai's increasing urbanity. Largely through advertisements, these periodicals, along with street billboards, purveyed modern images to a receptive audience of petty urbanites and consumers and helped shape their taste.

City life was growing richer by the day. Shanghai was the ultimate arena for actors, dancers, singers, musicians and other performing artists. The applause of *its* audience was what every performer wanted to hear. It was also where regional forms became more national. Originating in the folk music of Zhejiang province, the Yue (or Shaoxing) Drama widened its repertoire and technical range after its arrival in Shanghai around 1916, absorbing influences from Western-style drama and Peking Opera. From 1923 it came to be performed by all-female companies—the Yuesheng Girls' Yue Drama Troupe shown here being one example.

On June 9, 1931, a pageant rolled through Shanghai. The occasion was the dedication of the memorial temple Du Yuesheng had built to his ancestors in Pudong, on the other side of the Huangpu River. By the dazzle of the celebrations, Du was demanding Shanghai's recognition of his social arrival. In his social ascent, from small-time hood to pillar of respectable society, may be discerned the opportunity and mobility Shanghai offered to those with energy, an eye to the main chance and underworld connections.

At 11 pm on January 28, 1932, 400 Japanese marines headed for the heart of Zhabei, the district with the railway station to the north of the Suzhou Creek. Advancing along Sichuan Road North (*top*), the armoured division found itself resisted by a defence so spirited and heroic that the world had to revise its poor opinion of the Chinese soldier. Bombing by Japanese planes and shelling from Japanese guns and warships ushered in "a panorama sharp with images of horror and carnage." Under repeated attacks by Japanese marines (*right*), Zhabei was razed to the ground.

Residents of a devastated Zhabei found themselves homeless and prey to Japanese brutalities. They streamed into the International Settlement and the French Concession, neutral territory, clutching such things as they still possessed. The foreigners there watched the hostilities from afar and, because they viewed the Japanese as allies, were not only slow to condemn the atrocities but keen to take advantage of the Japanese attack to enlarge the Settlement. The foreigners' mouthpiece, the *North China Daily News*, said that "current controversies will not be allowed to prejudice Shanghai's treatment" of newly arrived Japanese soldiers.

One who knew what it was to be a refugee was this Russian taxi dancer, behind whose look of ennui lurked a desperate struggle for preservation. Forced to flee by the Bolshevik victory, many White Russians had fetched up in Shanghai. Could the taxi dancer have been snapped while waiting for a man to buy a book of tickets and use one on her? Say "White Russians" in Shanghai, and the image conjured up in most minds was of a bodyguard if male, or a dance hostess if female. Dispossessed, deprived of citizenship, socially they occupied a grey area between white expatriates and Chinese.

The Russian colony, 25,000 strong in 1934, was made up of Jewish and White Russian émigrés, some of whom had come straight from Siberia, and others after a sojourn in Harbin, in Manchuria, where they had fled after Vladivostok's fall to the Bolsheviks. Once a year they held a ball in the Majestic Hotel. Though regarded generally as inferiors by the other white communities, and only reluctantly trusted with responsible jobs, nevertheless the one thing everyone recognized was that in their way these émigrés were essential to the glamour and allure of Shanghai.

A night on the town might well take in a floor show performed by White Russian girls. Because of the arrival of White Russians, Shanghai had many more nightclubs and restaurants, more jazz and classical music, much more razzmatazz. Beef stroganoff, Chicken à la Kiev and *borsch* found their way into menus.

Shanghai's nightlife was "a whirligig of gaiety." "Joy, gin, and jazz. There's nothing puritanical about Shanghai," says a 1930s guidebook, which names Ladow's Cassanova, Venus Café, Vienna Ballroom, Palais Café and the Ambassador among the cabarets to be recommended. The largest, or so an advertisement claims, was the Majestic (whose Russian jazz orchestra is pictured here)—with "First-Class Floor and Catering—100 Charming Dance Hostesses."

Clubs were legion, offering diversions both social and sporting. There was boxing at the Sokols', the Russian sports club at 888 Weihaiwei Road (*top*). There was the Basque game *pelota*, or *Jai alai*, played at the Parc des Sports "Auditorium" on Avenue du Roi Albert, Shaanxi Road South today (*right*). The players banged a very hard ball against the three walls of the court with a hook-shaped basketwork glove. The tournaments offered ample opportunity to gamblers, and large bets were placed by the spectators. At first tournaments were held three, four times a week, then they became a daily occurrence.

A year after the Japanese attack, Shanghai wore the confidence that came from being certain of its identity and superiority. Its inhabitants, numbering a little under three and half million in 1933, were proud to call themselves Shanghainese whatever their origin. In the hiatus before another outbreak of war, the promenade of the Bund, pictured here overlooked by the Cathay Hotel tower in 1932–33, had a leisurely feel, caught in a moment of grace, or of pause.

The International Settlement was sheltered from man-made hazards but not natural ones. it is hard to drain Shanghai, which lies on the alluvial plain of the Yangtze Delta, with the ground water only five feet below the absolutely flat surface. In summer the city experienced many fierce typhoons, when ships were sometimes lost at sea. Despite good sewers the city would be flooded at these times, its trees uprooted and the Bund itself littered with the shipping that had been lifted up by the monsoon winds and deposited there.

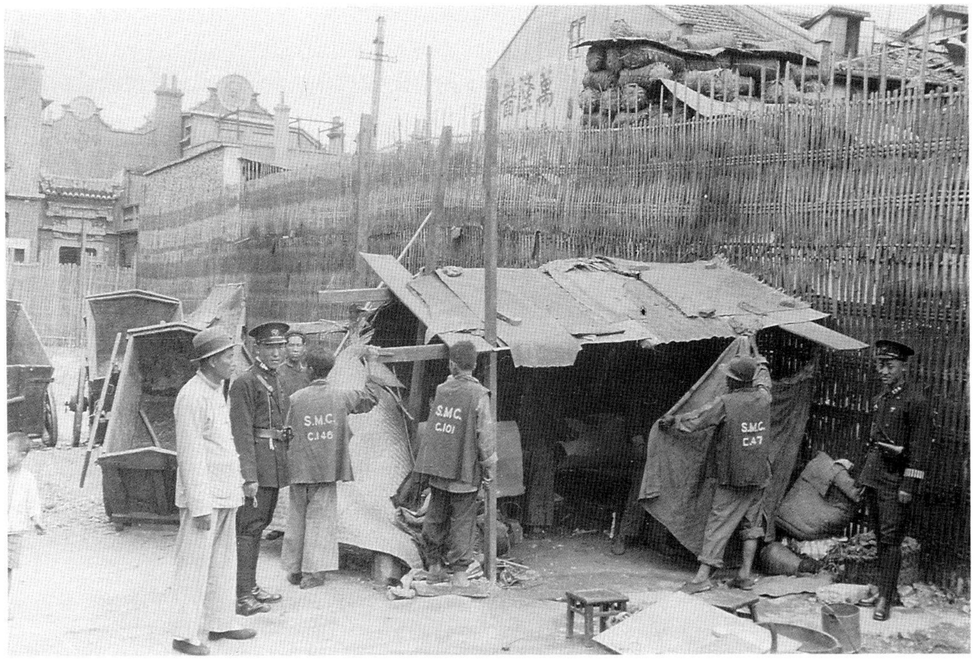

Sewage was part of the Shanghai Municipal Council's civic responsbilities. So were clearing squatter huts (*top*) and street cleaning. The picture on the left shows the Settlement's street sweepers at their duties with bamboo dustpans and reed brooms. They wore bright red cotton jackets and blue trousers, and a wide-brimmed straw hat with a broad red cotton band, both band and jacket emblazoned with the letters, S.M.C. (Shanghai Municipal Council).

For poor immigrants from the country, the squatter huts were a step up the residential ladder from the *maomao chuan*, "little hat boats," which had brought them to Shanghai. Many such "boat people" were to be found on the Suzhou Creek. The sail might then be used to make a low tunnel-shaped onshore shelter called *gundilong*. With some mud, reeds and bamboo added, these shelters became the squatter huts of the preceding page. The foreign residents described these as "beggar villages" and the boats as "beggar boats."

It was mostly migrants from northern Jiangsu province who lived in the squatter settlements, and it was these men too who did most of the rickshaw pulling—indeed, in the mid-1930s nine out of ten pullers of the 80,000 rickshaws in the streets of Shanghai were *Gaungpook ning*, the Shanghainese name for "northern Jiangsu people" that was also a pejorative rather like "yokel" or "boor."

Nightsoil is being loaded into boats at the "nightsoil jetty" in Hongkou. Every day the boats carried their liquid cargo from the city to some little country creek where a farmer waited for his manure, to be stored in huge earthenware jars until it was time to spread it on his crops. Shanghai nightsoil was particularly welcome, considered superior and especially fertile thanks to the rich diets of the people. A lucrative business, it was monopolized by a gangster's moll called Cassia Ma. To this day thousands of Shanghai households make do with chamberpots (made of wood and lidded), lacking flush toilets.

The nightsoil collector (*top*) was almost certainly a northern Jiangsu migrant, as were dustmen, bathhouse attendants (who doubled as pedicurists and masseurs) and barbers, for such lowly jobs were shunned by migrants from richer areas like Zhejiang. Like the blacks of New York or the Irish of London, northern Jiangsu people were generally treated as inferiors. A child barber plies his trade (*left*). Street barbers usually carried a shoulder pole with a washbasin at one end and a stool for the customer at the other.

Garden party to mark the inauguration of the Alliance Française, 1934. Chinese guests at such functions tended to be returned students from France: Zheng Yuxiu, the woman doctor of laws, for example, and Zhu Minyi, an eccentric athletics enthusiast who edited a popular health magazine and who was later to turn traitor. At the time the French, 2,500-strong, were greatly outnumbered by Anglo-Saxons: British (9,200) and American (3,800).

In 1934 the local gentry of Caojiadu, hard by whose slums lay the salubrious 45-acre campus of St. John's University, raised a memorial arch to honour its dedicated and influential president, the Rev. F.L. Hawks Pott (*centre*). It was under Pott that this American Christian university acquired its distinguished reputation. T.V. Soong and (Ambassador) Wellington Koo were just two of its many famous alumni.

The home of one British resident in Shanghai (*top*), and inside the home of another (*right*). The former, at 17 Crescent Avenue in the ICI (Imperial Chemical Industries) Compound, was the home from 1933 to 1942 of Hugh Collar, who was to end his career as vice-chairman of ICI in Hong Kong. British homes in Shanghai were comfortable enough, but Americans could sometimes be heard disdaining their plumbing and central heating.

Like any sojourning community, the British did their best to transplant the habits and pastimes of home—the St. Patrick Day's Ball, shooting, hunting and so on—and to turn Shanghai into a surrogate Surrey or Sussex. They set the tone of Shanghai's expatriate society. "It is appalling," observed an American, "what can happen to the average American housewife when she gets within hailing distance of what she thinks is high society, especially if it happens to have a British accent . . . It made my flesh crawl to hear American women go around imitating the la-di-da manners of the British . . ."

The foreigners enjoyed country walking and weekend "houseboating." "To obtain a houseboat, fully equipped and manned," reads a 1930s guide, "advertise in the local newspapers." An account left of an excursion up the Huangpu mentions "a sumptuous lunch, with plenty to drink, including vodka on draught from one of those glass jars the size of an acid carboy, generally used in all offices to contain iced drinking water."

A Chinese guest on a houseboat excursion would be rare, but still Shanghainese and foreigners were mixing on fairly easy terms, as this picture of a year-end party for the managerial staff of Texaco at the Xinghua Lou (Restaurant) shows. The American University Club had begun admitting Chinese members as far back as 1908—"No other club here," an American wrote, "is so free from racial prejudice." But Chinese were not allowed to join the American Club until 1929, and the (British) Shanghai Club until 1941.

One place where no colour bar seemed to prevail was the nightclub or cabaret. A contemporary guide tell us: "The 'dancing hostesses'—they amiably entertain at a dime to a dollar a dance; Russians, Chinese, Japanese, Koreans, Eurasians—occasionally others." The dance hostess stood in the line of the singsong girl, now seen to belong to an earlier, less modern, time. Instead of contesting for the title of "President of the Flowery Kingdom," the hostesses now vied to be "President of the Dance Kingdom."

Previously unquestioned ideas of sex, love and the status of women had been repeatedly challenged since the May Fourth Movement, though the rejection of tradition was an urban luxury, beyond the reach of rural women whose energies were consumed by just the struggle for survival. American educated, Soong Meiling (*front row, centre*) projected for many the image of modern Chinese womanhood. Here she poses with members of the Shanghai's women's movement which she publicly championed.

Yet feminism was disparaged in the 1934 New Life Movement, a social and moral clean-up campaign mixing Confucian, Christian and Fascist elements launched by Soong Meiling and her husband. Agitprop, films, posters, plays and lectures spread the word; and the Boy Scouts and the YMCA were sent to enforce it. Chastity was urged upon women. Casual sex, immodest clothing, spitting, flirting and smoking in public were condemned.

The New Life Movement's proscription of permed hair damaged the business of hairdressing salons, but not for long. Shanghai women were famously fashion-conscious—a term used of and by them was *shimao*, an addition to the Chinese lexicon coined from the English word "smart." The two side buns worn by girls in the pre-First World War period had long given way to bobbed hair, and thousands of women emerged from hairdressing salons sporting a permanent wave.

Extravagance was attacked by the New Life Movement and mass weddings were encouraged to eliminate the cost of separate celebrations. White bridal gowns inspired by Western example had come into fashion. As part of the changes wrought by modernization, since the beginning of the century ancient rites had given way to the so-called *wenming jiehun*, "civilized wedding ceremony," a form attacked by purists as "neither new nor old, neither Chinese nor Western, neither a horse nor a donkey."

The old existed alongside the new. Elaborately decorated old-style bridal sedans (*top*) and ostentatious funeral processions could still be seen in Shanghai's streets, their passage accompanied by music and fanfare. Wedding and funeral paraphernalia were chartered, from *shiqi* shops whose business it was to provide the necessary props. Coffins were customarily hung about with "condolence couplets" eulogizing the deceased (*left*).

Morning exercises at a Shanghai school (*top*) and children at a primary school (*right*). The idea of a tramp in the country would once have bemused most Chinese, strangers to the notion of physical exertion for its own sake; but now sports and physical training co-existed with classics and calligraphy. The 1920s and 1930s saw increasing convergence in classroom methods and content between Chinese and foreign mission schools, the latter now grown more secular.

Embrace of things foreign was far from total. A favoured instrument of resistance was the boycott, used on occasion against British, American and Japanese goods, the protests both patriotic and protectionist. In 1934, declared the *Guohuo* (National Merchandise) Year, indigenous manufacturers (such as the Five Continents Pharmaceutical Company pictured here) promoted their products in sound trucks and displays. Selling a popular local speciality, Longhua peaches (*left*), a hawker was photographed by Robert Vyvyan Dent of the family that established Dent & Company.

Western retailers were no match for overseas Chinese department stores like Sincere, founded like the Wing On (*page 81*) by a Cantonese clan (Ma) with Australian connections. Competition from rival emporia—Sun Sun and Dai Sun as well as Wing On, the so-called "big four"—was met by such Western ploys as seasonal sales, lucky draws, free gifts and coupons. Sincere was not only a retail outlet but a place of relaxation and diversion, its famous roof garden offering music and other forms of entertainment.

The department store was at one end of the retail range; the *yanzhi* ("tobacco and paper") shop was at the other. These small shops were set in or near the entrance to lanes and catered to the everyday needs of the local residents. They were your friendly neighbourhood corner shops and their patrons were entirely Chinese. The poster to the left of the picture advertises a bedbug killer.

Catering to a higher stratum of society was the Siberian Fur Store (*top*), a name still heard in Hong Kong today. That and the art decoration store pictured here (*right*) were just two of the many speciality shops opened by Shanghai's Russian community. By starting dress salons and beauty parlours the Russians brought a sense of European style to the city. Many Russians had their shops and homes on Avenue Joffre, which for that reason was known as Little Russia or Nevsky Prospekt.

Also run by Russians was the Viener Sausage Factory on Route Dollfus, Nanchang Road today (*top*), a reminder that this was a city of niche economies, linked by ethnic and cultural ties to societies for away. The Russian–owned bookshop on Avenue Joffre (*left*) was a reminder that by 1937 more Russian books were published in Shanghai than in Berlin or Paris. The city supported two Russian newspapers, the *Shanghai Zaria* (*Shanghai Dawn*) and *Slovo* (the *Word*) as well as a large number of literary clubs.

The wealth of service trades was part of the city's character. The efflorescence of new recreational venues was one reason for the eventual decline of Qingliange (*top*) on Fuzhou Road, once the haunt of cultivated society, with a teahouse above and an amusement arcade below. Shanghai's biggest tea merchant was Wang Yutai (*right*), whose head office was at 197 Avenue Foch and which had four branches by 1935.

One frequented the teahouse for storytelling and balladry and theatres like the Lyceum for stage plays and, from 1931 onwards, movies. The old Lyceum (*page 15*) had been rebuilt at a new address, today's Maoming Road South, in the French Concession. The Chinese stage play, or New Drama as the locals called it, was a domesticated Western import pioneered in Shanghai. After its heyday in the early 1920s, it went into a decline until its reappearance in a new, more professional guise as *huaju*, "spoken drama."

Many theatregoers were simultaneously Western-style drama fans and Peking Opera enthusiasts. Shanghai loved Mei Lanfang (1894–1961) and his female impersonations in celebrated Peking Operas like *The Drunken Beauty* and *Beauty Defies Tyranny*—loved him all the more for his patriotic refusal to sing for the Japanese after the outbreak of war. It lapped up popular press reports of him meeting Konstantin Stanislavsky and Bertolt Brecht, and Charlie Chaplin, Douglas Fairbanks and Mary Pickford in Hollywood.

The Shanghainese thrilled to Hollywood movies and packed cinemas like the Crystal Palace, Star, Grand, Cathay, Ritz, Metropole, Carlton and Nanking (pictured here showing *Tarzan* in 1935). It was in Shanghai, in the course of a variety show at the Xu Gardens, that Chinese audiences saw their first movie. Movie houses grew fastest between 1926 and 1932, a period when Shanghai's own film industry got into its stride. The best ones showed American movies, whose stars became Shanghainese idols.

Shanghai, with as many as 50 homegrown studios between 1928 and 1931, well deserved the epithet the "Haolaiwu [Hollywood] of the East." Among the most important were Mingxing (Star) and Lianhua, makers of some of the finest movies in Chinese history, movies that were as good as any made in the West at the time. These films' seriousness came of the leftwing penetration of the studios and the patriotism, fanned by Japanese aggression, of the directors and scenario writers.

No Chinese film actress could hold a candle to Ruan Lingyu, the great silent movie star who, so wrote an American film historian, was "as perfectly and peculiarly adapted to the film as we recognize Greta Garbo to be." Her portrayal of a novelist who commits suicide in *New Women* (*left*) moves the heart and caused a sensation when it opened in February 1935. On 8 March, she herself took her own life. She was 25. The other still (*right*) is from *Life* (1934).

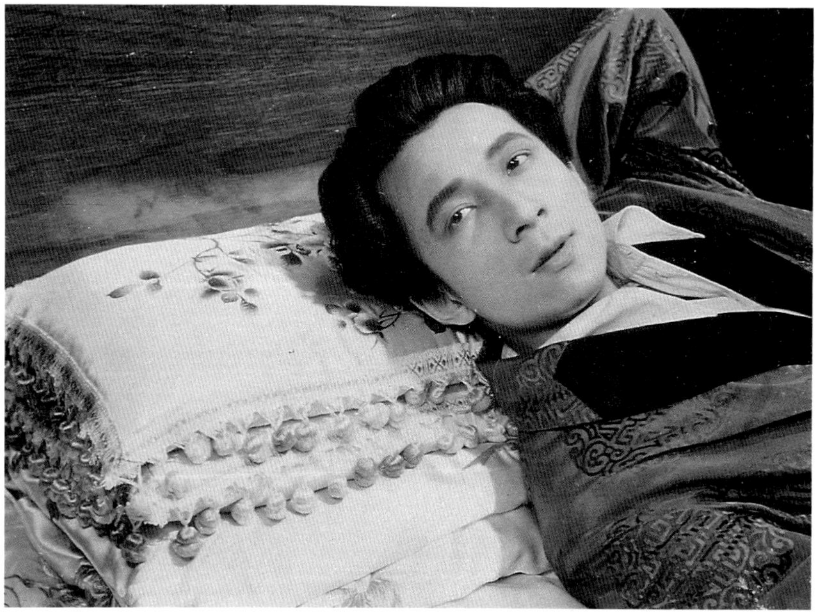

Shanghai, more extravagantly than any other city, offered the prizes of showbiz fame. But unlike Ruan Lingyu, Lan Ping (*top*) never made it there. In 1937 she went to Yanan, the revolutionary base, and two years later married Mao Zedong. In her post-1949 incarnation, as Jiang Qing, she persecuted film figures who had outshone her in Shanghai. Yuan Muzhi (*right*), too, was to rise in the political hierarchy—to become the head of the film bureau—but from having first distinguished himself as an actor and, more importantly, as the director of the classics *Street Angel* and *Scenes of City Life*.

Students in the Department of Western Painting (one of four, the others being Chinese Painting, Graphic Design and Music) at the Shanghai School of Art (Shanghai Meishu Zhuanke Xuexiao). Founded in 1912 by famous painters like the French-trained Liu Haisu, it taught the history of European painting from the Renaissance down to the Impressionists and pioneered the use of nude models in life drawing classes. A 1919 exhibition featuring a female nude painting by Liu caused an uproar, but by the 1930s the Shanghainese were taking such paintings in their stride.

The first Chinese musicians to play European instruments, like the first Chinese to paint in the Western idiom, were nurtured on Shanghai soil. Among the many achievements of the great educationalist Cai Yuanpei was the establishment of the National Music College in the French Concession in 1927. European musical life in Shanghai was further enriched by the influx of Jewish refugees from Nazism in 1938–39. The gifted musicians among them played in the Shanghai Municipal Orchestra and taught at the Shanghai Conservatory.

An attack by the Japanese on July 7, 1937 near the Marco Polo Bridge in Peking marked the start of the Second World War. On Friday, August 13, the first shots were fired and the siege of Shanghai began. The next day, Bloody Saturday, Chiang Kaishek ordered his airforce to bomb the Japanese warships anchored off Shanghai's docks. But the bombs missed the Japanese fleet and instead hit the city, killing hundreds of civilians (*top*). To fleeing refugees (*left*), Shanghai as always beckoned like an island of safety.

Many foreign residents opted for evacuation—"The little word embraced so much: lost face, lost hope, a lost city." The white man's day was over. Zhabei was put to the torch. Fleeing Japanese bombs and bullets, a mass exodus from Hongkou and Yangshupu poured across Garden Bridge into the International Settlement, swelling its population from 1.6 million to possibly five million or more. Refugee camps sprouted, but such was the destitution that 101,047 exposed corpses were picked up during the following year.

Japan began secretly to offer Chiang Kaishek peace terms to consider. Germany agreed to act as mediator (it would suit her well enough to see the Japanese armies deflected to the Soviet Union), and her emissaries worked behind the scenes to get negotiations under way. Chiang would not budge, however, despite the efforts of Oscar Trautmann (*centre*), the German Ambassador in Nanking, pictured here arriving in Shanghai on November 28 on one of his three missions. From Shanghai he went on to Nanking on December 20 to exert renewed pressure on Chiang.

While the foreign enclaves remained neutral territory, the Chinese parts of Shanghai were now under Japanese occupation. The Japanese sentries stationed on Garden Bridge, the uniformed Japanese at the Yangshupu Police Station (*top*), and the inspection of those entering the dock area in Hongkou (*right*) were all reminders of Japanese military aggrandizement. The army's Special Service section now worked to set up governments which, though ostensibly Chinese, took their orders from the Japanese military.

The Special Service handed the administration of Chinese Shanghai to the puppet Dadao (Great Way) Municipal Government on December 5, 1937. Here the government's troops are shown marching past the Jiangwan civic centre in a celebration marking its reorganization one year later as the Special Municipality of Shanghai. The puppet mayor, Fu Xiaoan, was later found hacked to death in his sleep. By then Wang Jingwei, Kuomintang stalwart turned collaborator, had been installed at 1126 Yuyuan Road prior to setting up a national collaborationist government.

With the Japanese all about its borders, the Settlement was now called Gudao, "Solitary Island." It was unoccupied, but by no means immune to Japanese expansionism. One form this took was the seizure of Chinese administrative organs located within the foreign enclaves—the Chinese Telegraph Administration, the Wireless Administration, and the Chinese General Post Office (whose building, raised in 1924, is pictured here overlooking Sichuan Road North).

Clearly the Japanese had designs upon the foreign enclaves. The Westerners did not stand up to them but instead surrendered more and more of their authority. In 1940, France fell; and that autumn the new French Consul–General, R J de Margerie, brought the French Concession under the jurisdiction of the Vichy Government. The sheen was to wear off Avenue Joffre, perhaps the concession's most famous street.

In the grounds of 10 Avenue Pétain, life was reassuringly gracious and civilized, for all the gathering clouds of World War II. The Shanghai American School was founded in 1912 and moved to its Ave Pétain campus in 1923. To this day its alumni in America celebrate its anniversary. The graduating class pictured here was photographed on June 13, 1940. The Japanese bombardment of Pearl Harbor was a year and a half away.

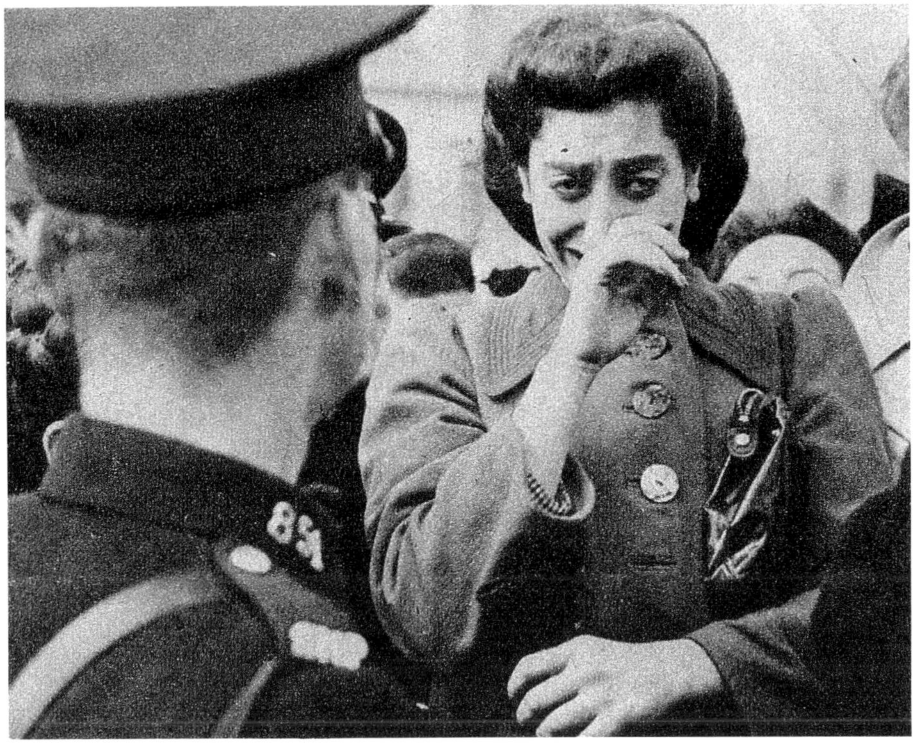

Friends and relatives—and a tearful woman—saw off a platoon of the US Marines from the Bund in November 1941. From 1937 to 1941, China fought alone. It was Pearl Harbor that made America's full involvement in the war certain. Chiang Kaishek's government rejoiced at the American commitment, envisioning greatly augmented American aid.

At 10 a.m. sharp on December 8, 1941, the Japanese army entered the Settlement. With the Japanese declaration of war on the United States and Great Britain, the Far Eastern war and the European war coalesced into a world war. The Japanese flag was raised over the Hongkong and Shanghai Bank on the Bund (*right*). Crowds surrounded the statue of Sir Robert Hart as Japanese soliders began tearing it down (*top*). Other monuments they demolished were the Angel of Victory on the World War I memorial and the statue of the British diplomat Sir Harry Parkes, erected on the Bund in 1890.

The red armband worn by the European pedestrian (*top*) proclaimed which of the Allied nationalities he was—"A" for America, "B" for Britian, "H" for Holland and "X" for other nationalities. Without such armbands enemy aliens were barred from racecourses, cinemas, theatres, nightclubs and so on. Presently they were interned, in camps such as the one on Haiphong Road (*left*), to which Hugh Collar (*second from right*), Chairman of the British Residents' Association, was sent in November 1942 and where he remained for two and a half years.

March 10, 1943 was the thirty-eighth anniversary of Japan's shattering defeat of Russia in the war of 1904–5. So as not to ruffle any Soviet feathers (it would be another two years before the USSR entered the Pacific war), the army of occupation commemorated it in another guise, as the Japanese Navy Day. The International Settlement where commemorative banners hung was no longer a foreign enclave—the Western treaty powers had renounced their rights to it in January. The Western interlude was over.

"Peaceful National Construction," reads a pennant over a propaganda performance (*left*). This was a slogan of the Wang Jingwei government, allowed in July and August 1943 to assume administrative control of the International Settlement and the French Concession—the foreign enclaves had been swept away, the Western treaty powers having relinquished their rights to them in January. In a public relations exercise in April, a song and dance ensemble sent by Japan in April performed at the Nanking Theatre (*page 123*). The three characters (*top*) form part of "The Greater East Asia Co-prosperity Sphere," an enlargement of the "New Order."

Opium dens, called "swallows' nests" in the vernacular, were concentrated in Jiumoudi in the Chinese City (around today's Dajing Road and Luxiangyuan Road). The one pictured here disguised itself as an addiction treatment centre (*top*). Brothels were concentrated in Huile Li, "Lane of Gathered Happiness," off Fuzhou Road (*right*). Japanese-sponsored racketeering and extortion schemes balefully boosted opium smoking and prostitution. Crime and corruption were rampant under the occupation.

Victory came. Shops in a jubilant Shanghai closed for a day on August 11 to celebrate. The US Fleet (seen here from the southern end of the Bund) was welcomed like a promise of great times. Soon thousands of American soldiers and marines were billeted in the city. The Huangpu bristled with American warships and supply vessels. American dollars here, as elsewhere, went a long way. Britain was no longer number one in Shanghai. Preparations would soon be afoot for a switch from left to right hand drive.

A street fortune teller divined the future surrounded by men who, as is the way with people in the clutch of despair, were living just for today (*top*). They had survived the worst that alien occupation could do to them, but would they survive the wild inflation that now threatened to reduce them to destitution? Between September 1945 and May 1946, wholesale prices increased elevenfold. The ordinary people, such as the men in this humble teashop (*right*), were engaged in a perpetual struggle against both wartime and peacetime attrition.

Writers, artists and intellectuals regrouped in Shanghai. Many had long been radicalized by the communist underground; indeed the partriotic/revolutionary cause was now the very basis of salon and cultural life. None of the luminaries—scenarist Yu Ling (*seated, far right*), playwright and scriptwriter Tian Han (*seated, second from right*), actor and scenarist Ouyang Yuqian (*seated, far left*), and opera star Zhou Xinfang (*standing, sixth from left*)—among the film and theatre people gathered here lacked political conviction.

The post–World War II period was marked by hunger riots, workers' strikes and student protest, for the most part communist-inspired. The students' rallying cries were "independence," "freedom," "democracy" and—as pictured here—"We want peace not war!" They agitated against famine, "American imperialism" and an end to the civil war. Chiang Kaishek's government retaliated with arrests, prohibitions and conciliations.

In 1948–49 Shanghai was "a city in reprieve, living off foreign subsidies." The spring of 1949 marked a waiting period in the city. Many Europeans left, including Catholic priests and nuns. Word had reached them that the advancing communist troops dealt harshly with Christian missionaries, killing from 60 to 100 between 1946 and 1948. In Shanghai the Western population plunged from 65,409 in 1946 to 28,683 in November 1949, the year of the communist takeover.

The communists were riding the tide of history. Chiang Kaishek had said that he would hold the Nanking and Shanghai region to the bitter end, but then decamped to Taiwan. The last days passed. In a beleaguered Shanghai citizens and Kuomintang soldiers and civilians awaited word of the advancing People's Liberation Army (*top*). After token resistance, Shanghai fell. Many Shanghainese only knew because they read about it in the papers (*right*); others woke on May 25, 1949 to see white flags waving on buildings.

Soldiers of the People's Liberation Army march down the Bund. "I had," wrote a diplomat, "expected to see tough, weather-beaten, fire-eating soldiers." But they were "mostly teenagers in the first blush of youth" or "almost adult country bumpkins . . . looking around open-eyed, obviously bewildered by the ornate and magnificent buildings of the city." They had neither the courage of a Humphrey Bogart, he said, nor the suavity of an Errol Flynn.

Loudspeakers hailed the deliverance of Shanghai from "traitors, oppressors, cruel capitalist exploiters and iron–heeled imperialists" in a liberation parade in which military units of the People's Liberation Army marched through the streets with workers and other citizens. The parade, sporting pictures of Mao Zedong, put a seal on the communist takeover of Shanghai. For the next 40 years, the communists would contrive new roles and realities for it, until they restored it to its original purposes by reopening Shanghai to the wider world.

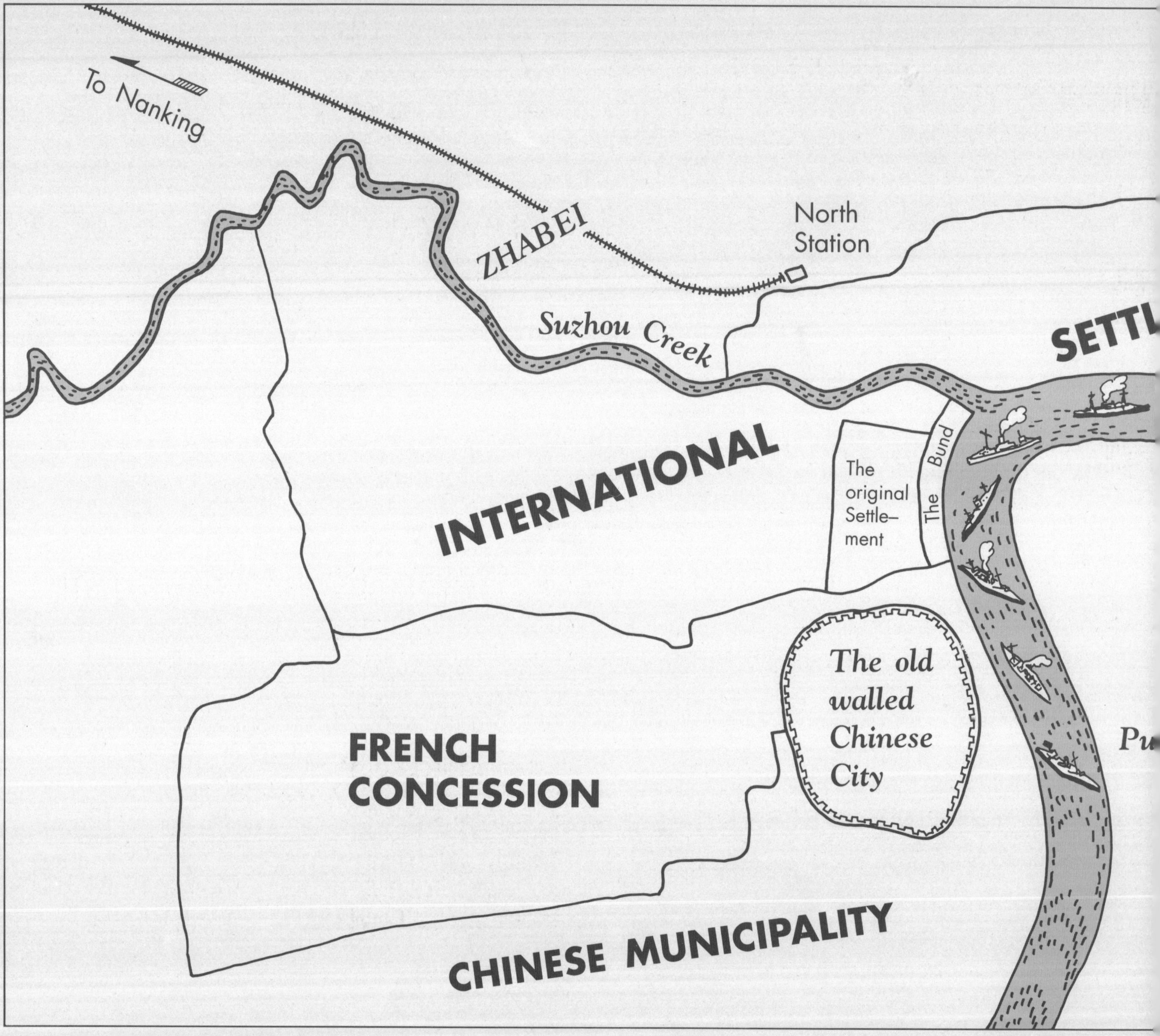
To Nanking
ZHABEI
North Station
Suzhou Creek
SETTL
INTERNATIONAL
The original Settle–ment
The Bund
The old walled Chinese City
FRENCH CONCESSION
Pu
CHINESE MUNICIPALITY